The Deer

Story by
ANITA TOWNSEND

Pictures by
BERNARD ROBINSON

Angus & Robertson · Publishers

The little calf lay quietly where his mother had left him, hidden in a clump of bracken. He had been born only two hours before, but already he could stand up. His mother was feeding in a clearing not far away. The calf blinked at a butterfly dancing in the sunlight above his head and twitched his soft ears. All he could hear was the distant tap of a woodpecker and the drone of a bee among the bluebells.

Then a blackbird flew up with a cry of alarm. The calf crouched down in his bed of bracken and, peering through the fronds, saw a wild pig. Behind her trotted a string of snorting piglets. The calf was too weak to run away, so he kept very still. None of the pigs saw the calf, nor did they smell him for his scent was very weak because he was so young.

In the evening the calf's mother came back to feed him. He stood up on his shaky legs and thrust his head under her belly to suck her warm milk. When night fell they lay down close together. An owl drifted silently overhead, looking for mice, but the little calf was not afraid. He listened to his mother quietly chewing the cud of grass that she had eaten earlier, and he nestled up against her warm fur.

Suddenly, a little way off in the dark, they
heard the bark of a fox, followed by a frightened
squeak, then a rustle among the leaves and a
sharp cry. A fox had found a young hare and
killed it. The calf and his mother lay hidden and
still. At last the fox finished his meal and they
heard him slink away.

As the summer days passed the calf grew quickly. He played with the other calves born in the herd that year. There were only calves and females, called hinds, in the herd. The male deer, the stags, lived in a different part of the forest.

The calves ran about together, chased and butted each other and reared up on their hind legs to box with their slender forelegs. One of their favourite games was to race together to a mound or fallen tree; one would jump to the top, then they would all race away again.

One day the calves were playing in an open glade when a cold shadow swept across the grass. The old hind who was the leader of the herd gave a sharp bark of alarm. The calf looked up and saw a buzzard wheeling over the glade. The old hind headed swiftly for the trees and all the other hinds and calves followed her in single file along the forest track. Soon they were all safe under the trees.

Autumn and winter passed. By the time spring came again the calf had stopped drinking his mother's milk. He ate leaves and grass, for he was now no longer a calf, he was a young stag.

He stayed with the herd of hinds and calves throughout the long, drowsy summer; but as autumn approached he began to feel restless. He heard the stags, the big males, bellowing through the autumn mists. One morning, when a frost had stiffened the grass, he saw one of the beasts for the first time. With its dark shaggy mane and its branching antlers, it came boldly into the forest glade where the hinds and young were feeding.

The young stag looked up with fear as the big male stared and snorted. Its breath hung white in the frosty air. Then the animal lowered its head and wheeled round, turning its great antlers towards the young stag.

Frightened, the young one ran away into the trees. He ran without stopping until the sun was high in the sky. He was too far away now to go back to the herd. When he came to a river he scrambled down the rocky bank, plunged into the cold water and swam across. He wandered alone through the forest for several days. Then he met a herd of young males like himself who allowed him to join them. The young stag lived with them, away from the older stags and the hind herds, until he was a full grown stag.

One fine spring morning the stag made his way to a boggy pool by the river. Here he lay down and rolled and wallowed and rubbed his sides against tussocks of reed and grass. He was now six years old and he had grown into a big strong stag with wide branching antlers. He no longer needed his thick winter coat; his skin felt hot and prickly in the warm spring sunshine and the cool mud and water was soothing. When he climbed out of the wallowing-hole he was black and dripping with mud. He rubbed himself against the rough trunk of a tree to get rid of tufts of loose hair.

That evening, as the sun was sinking, the
stag walked down to the river to drink. A squirrel
chattered in the branches overhead. The stag
looked up and there was a sudden sharp crack as
one of his antlers knocked against a bough. The
antler broke off and fell to the ground. Startled,
the stag bounded away, but he was not hurt.

Soon his second antler fell off and the stag was left with two little stumps. But the stumps felt hot and tender. They throbbed and swelled and then they started to grow. By the end of the summer they had grown into new antlers that were even bigger than the old ones. They were covered with soft velvety fur. The stag took care not to knock against anything lest he hurt them.

When his new antlers had grown to their full size the velvety skin that covered them began to harden and peel off in strips. The strips of dry skin hanging about his head irritated the stag, so he dug his antlers into the earth and rubbed them against the trees to clean them.

As the autumn drew near he grew fat and sleek and heavy. He had been feeding on the rich summer grass and leaves. His neck swelled and his mane grew thick. He often went to his wallowing-place away from the other stags to lie in the mud and cool himself.

The leaves of the forest turned to gold, and the nights grew frosty although the days were still bright and sunny. The stag grew more and more restless as the days grew shorter. He moved away from the summer feeding grounds and went in search of the hind herds.

After wallowing in a boggy pool one evening he lay down to rest and chew the cud. He flicked and twitched his ears, listening to every sound that came from the forest. The roar and grunting cough of another stag rang through the trees. The stag raised his muzzle and bellowed a reply. Then he set off towards the noise he had heard. He burst out of the woods into a clearing and saw ahead of him, across the grass, another stag, older than himself, with a herd of hinds and calves.

The stag advanced towards the herd. When he got close he stopped and pawed at the earth; he dug his sharp antlers into the turf and threw clods of earth over his back. He did not dare attack the other stag straight away; but he wanted to frighten it and show it how strong he was. The older stag tossed its antlers and snorted.

Suddenly, both stags lowered their heads and charged. Their great antlers crashed and locked together. They snorted and grunted and tore up the clods of earth under their hooves as they struggled. Then the stag gathered his back legs under his belly, bent his back, and lunged forward with all his weight. The other animal staggered back a few paces but recovered itself. Then it heaved itself with such force against its rival that both stags were almost knocked off their feet. They regained their balance and drew apart, panting.

The animals roared at each other, pawed at the ground, then lunged to the attack again. The woods echoed with the crash of antlers. When their antlers were locked together, the stag suddenly swung his head sideways. He felt the other stag stumble and leapt forward. He stabbed at the animal's flanks with the sharp brow points of his antlers. Defeated, it jumped out of his way and then cantered off. It was not hurt, but it was beaten. The younger stag was the master now. He turned to look at the hinds he had won. Next day he would mate with some of them.

The stag had to guard his hinds now.
Whenever another stag came near he roared and
drove it away. He galloped round and round the
hinds to protect them and keep them together. He
did not want any of them to stray away or be
stolen by another stag. No other stag dared to
attack him, but even a small stag would try to
steal a few hinds if he was not looking.

After ten days the stag was thin and
exhausted. He had mated with most of his hinds
now. He went away to rest and feed and recover
before winter fell. He would pay no more
attention to the hinds that year; but, when the
spring came, the hinds he had mated with would
give birth to his calves, hidden deep in the leafy
greenwood.

Deer Facts

Sharp ears

Keen sense of smell

Long neck helps the deer reach tasty leaves and shoots.

The stag has six points on its antlers which shows he is full grown. He is called a royal stag.

Mane grows long in the mating season

The male (right) and female red deer

There are more than 50 kinds of deer, ranging in size from the North American moose (known as an elk in Europe) which is bigger than a horse to the tiny pudu of South America which is as small as a corgi dog. The red deer in the story lives in forests over almost all of Europe. It stands up to one and a half metres high at the shoulder with a long neck. The stag's (male's) antlers are over a metre long. The hind (female) is smaller and has no antlers.

Growing Antlers

The stag's antlers do not grow to their full size until the stag is six years old. Every spring they fall off, leaving behind two bony stumps called pedicles. As soon as the antlers have been shed, skin forms over the pedicles and, inside this, new antlers begin to grow.

After several months, the antlers are fully grown. They are covered in soft, furry skin, called velvet. Soon this peels, leaving shiny, polished bone. Then the stag is ready to mate.

Mating Time

For most of the year, the stags and hinds live apart from each other. But in autumn, each stag joins a group of hinds. The stags often have to fight with rivals to gain mastery of a herd. Their antlers look like truly dangerous weapons but in fact they protect the stags from severe injury. When the animals charge each other, the antlers become en-tangled and prevent their heads be-ing harmed. A sharp blow elsewhere is not so serious.

The stags also use their antlers to protect the hinds they have won. When the mating season is over, the antlers fall off.

The Hunter's Prey

Despite the frightening look of their antlers, deer are peaceful, rather timid animals. Deer fawns are often killed by foxes and wild cats. But the older ones have no real enemies but man. Once they were killed by the bears, lions and wolves that shared their forests. But most of these

Deers' hooves are split down the middle into two 'dew claws'

Deer Watch

Red deer are so shy that it is hard to get close to them. But if you look carefully you may see the signs they leave behind them, such as their footprints. You can tell these by the split down the middle. Deer also sometimes eat the bark of trees. So watch out for them when you see a tree with the bark stripped from the lower part of the trunk. Be patient and quiet and you may be lucky. Also, look out for antlers, but do not be surprised if you never find one; stags usually eat their antlers after they have shed them. This gives them the nourishment needed to grow new ones.

flesh-eaters have now been wiped out by man.

Man has always hunted deer; not just to display antlers as a trophy but also for food (venison). Because deer have few natural enemies, their numbers often increase so much that they damage trees and farm crops in their search for food. Foresters then have to hunt them to check the numbers. This 'culling' stops the deer population becoming so large that they starve to death.

Man's Friend

The reindeer is the only type of deer which is bred to help man. In the cold, snowy wastes of the Arctic it is more useful than a horse because it can survive extreme cold and find its way even in a snowstorm. The Lapps of Scandinavia live closely with the deer; they eat its flesh, drink its milk and make clothes and tents from its skin.

early spring late spring early summer late summer

The stag's antlers fall off and grow again each year.
It takes six years for them to reach full size.

More books for you to read from
ANGUS & ROBERTSON

WILDLIFE LIBRARY

If you have enjoyed this book, you will be pleased to know that it is part of a series:

The Tiger
0 207 95819 X

The Wolf
0 207 95843 2

The Kangaroo
0 207 95820 3

The Bear
0 207 95844 0

The Penguin
0 207 95821 1

The Elephant
0 207 95845 9

The Beaver
0 207 95822 X

The Deer
0 207 95846 7

EYE-VIEW LIBRARY

In addition, there are ten titles in the Eye-View Library, a companion series about the smaller creatures of the countryside:

The Song Thrush
0 207 95695 2

The Butterfly
0 207 95709 6

The Hedgehog
0 207 95693 6

The Fox
0 207 95772 X

The Bumblebee
0 207 95694 4

The Mouse
0 207 95773 8

The Squirrel
0 207 95710 X

The Duck
0 207 95832 7

The Frog
0 207 95708 8

The Otter
0 207 95833 5

All the books are in full colour.